# DISCOVERING

## BIBLICAL TRUTH,

### UNCOVERING GOD'S FAITH

Michael A. Bonilla, Ph.D.

FOREWORD BY
JACK HASHIM

Llumina Press

ISBN:   1-59526-247-4
Printed in the United States of America by Llumina Press

Library of Congress Control Number: 2004093678

# *Dedication*

## Ron and Mary Nell Wyatt

# Contents

# *Foreword*

Success does not come from a single idea, lucky break or a brilliant strategy. Each one of these advantages does not last forever. No, the foundation of a great work is more closely associated with the authors attributes. These attributes found in my friend Michael Bonilla, were active long before this book of poetry was written. You will discover as I have, that the ultimate success of this book had little to do with strategy, luck or a great idea. Michael willingly exposes his inner man without trace of masquerade. Dr. Michael Bonilla receives acclaim as a dedicated archaeologist. His ruggedness working with his gentleness illuminates an attribute known as balance.

I ask, "Why would an archaeologist write a book on poetry?" I found the answer written on the pages of this book. The purpose of this book offered value and endurance. The value of life and the enduring purpose of it are on every page. The poems will challenge you just as I have been challenged and I am thankful of it. The values originate from deep within the man. The authentic soul searching truths which Michael holds so dearly are expressed in rhyme. Most important, the anthology of poems will provide inspiration and even answers to some of life's questions. Spiritual truths are found on every page.

If the authors intent to stimulate the reader to a higher value and purpose of life, then he has succeeded. I sense within the man and his words, an unceasing drive and desire to bring about change in us and himself. There is a spiritual world out there which needs to be explored. As you search for it, many roadblocks will appear. To overcome obstacles, would be gain. The poems will help in guiding us through the enemies mine fields. It can be accomplished if we're willing to change; especially in our thought process. Relax! Enjoy the unique style and flexibility of words, while Michael spans generations through time.

The very act of writing these poems demonstrates Michael Bonilla's desire to share his wisdom. I feel many will prosper due to the passion released in this work. Be prepared for change, especially in areas of your life which you felt were fixed forever. To that I would say, "don't be afraid of change." I have discovered it is a rare ability to change while maintaining continuity with time. Here is the product of what a man can deliver after connecting the natural with the supernatural.

It may appear that we have in Michael Bonilla, a man who vacillates from delicate inspiration to bitter condemnation. This is no easy task; be prepared to be shaken from slumber. I can't deny that some poems are unorthodox but truly beautiful. There will be moments when what you read will be soothing to the spirit. He also writes with a scorch pen.

Open your understanding concerning warfare between the spiritual and natural worlds which surround us. I appreciate the art form expressed in Michael's book. Symbolism combined with faith inspired poetry is a major contribution in this book.

Repeatedly a common message is carried in various ways. What is that message? In a nutshell, this is the message, "If human relationships are wrong, no other factor of life can really matter." If love departs and friendships wither, in what way can man coexist? There are many warnings here. However, he is not preachy; nor does he give the appearance of being a specific crusade. Every thought is conveyed clearly and completely. I was thrilled by the many times Michael speaks of the ugly and the beautiful. It may be pointed out that Mr. Bonilla combines vivid perception of spiritual reality with an exquisite collection of devotional poetry.

I sensed at times, the emotions expressed were almost too large for words. Yet, they have been written and we will treasure them. Thank you, Michael.

Our friendship is my blessing.

Jack Hashim, 2004

# DISCOVERING

## BIBLICAL TRUTH,

### UNCOVERING GOD'S FAITH

# A JUDAS GENERATION

As God will always have a chosen generation that He's set apart,
for His heavenly wisdom and vast knowledge He wants to impart.
As the Glory of the Lord throughout the planet, He has revealed,
for unto repentance He has called us, as He continues to appeal.

The Judas generation is the one that knows God but rejects Him,
they choose to live a life full of iniquity while swimming in sin.
It's a generation of vipers who seek to discredit the Lord's glory,
the reality of Jesus is considered to be the world's greatest story.

A Judas generation seeks to glorify unto themselves continually,
for this generation of demonic lifestyle was not birth accidentally.
They lust after the flesh, as sin has become their sole habitation,
the Judas generation seeks to duplicate, such a transformation.

The hearts of men by their own free will, refuse to obey the Lord,
God is about to award the Judas generation with a terrible reward.
The Lord God will cause that generation to suffer great frustration,
if they don't repent in their hearts, they won't experience salvation.

# A MAN BY THE NAME OF SAMSON

From the day Samson was born until the time of his death,
a Nazarite unto God, spoken from the Lord's own breath.
The Spirit of the Lord would mightily come upon Samson,
as the Philistines had held the nation of Israel for ransom.

As the Philistines were seeking Samson; with hatred they pursued,
on that day Samson with a jawbone of an ass, a thousand men he slew.
For Samson judged Israel in the days of the Philistines twenty years,
but one day the LORD would cause Samson's strength to disappear.

For Samson had broken his Nazarite vows and sinned against the LORD,
but the day was coming, were the LORD would Samson's strength restore.
Oh' the Philistines thought their god Dagon, brought Samson to his knees,
but the LORD, who sought an occasion against the Philistines would seize.

But one day, Samson's hair began to grow, again after he was shaven,
for a day was coming when the Philistines would not have a safe haven.
As Samson was brought into Dagon's house while he was made sport,
taken to both pillars by the hand of a lad, his help he would resort.

Samson called and prayed to the LORD for strength, one more time,
to be avenged of the Philistines, his humiliation was their evil crime.
Samson held of the two middle pillars, upon which the house stood,
as the house fell upon the lords, and the people, death to all he slew.

# A MOTHER'S LOVE

A mother's love can never be measured,
her warmth is such a wonderful treasure.
Into this lost and dying world was I born,
greater love has no woman ever shown.

My mother's heart loves without condition,
her love has given me perfect nutrition.
She's been God's greatest gift to my life,
I'm so grateful for her, that I am alive.

A mother's love knows heavenly kindness,
for her virtue and grace are full of richness.
With love she has so carefully nurtured me,
while preparing me to face life, not sparingly.

My mother's children have always been her first priority,
through devotion and love while displaying her authority.
This godly woman that God had pre-ordained into my life,
has protected me through this world infested with strife.

# A PRICELESS TREASURE

There are many things that we would believe as priceless,
often, we give greater value to things considered worthless.
God's only son suffered for our sins as He died on the cross,
As Jesus for three days, became His Father's greatest loss.

Jesus is the priceless treasure, as He laid His life down,
He humbled Himself and willfully laid down His crown.
As the greatest act of love the world has ever witnessed,
for thirty three years, Jesus lived a life that was sinless.

The Ark of the Covenant is the greatest earthly treasure known,
for it symbolized at one time, God's residence and earthly throne.
The Ark's meaning at this dispensation of time, is such a treasure,
it's natural and historical value, makes it impossible to measure.

The Bible mentions the parable of the treasure that was hidden,
as for the Ark of the Covenant, from man's view it is forbidden.
That hidden treasure refers only to Jesus, our Savior and Lord,
for He is the true priceless treasure, that I worship and adore.

# A PROPHETIC WORD TO THE AUTHOR

At Glory Zone Fellowship, where I first received this prophetic word,
God spoke through my pastor, such awesome word, I did not deserve!
It was when God's calling, choosing and anointing came into my life,
as Jesus took me out of the darkness, and brought me into the light!

*And even as thou art an archaeologist, seeking out natural landmarks,*
*I am even causing thee to be an archaeologist of the Glory of God.*
*A connoisseur of the anointing, one that could flow in the spirit,*
*and discern and war in the Spirit. Prophesy, prophesy to the four winds!*
*For thou art a Warrior, thou art My gladiator,*
*thou art My black belt in the spirit... saith the Lord.*
*I will give thee dreams, oh man of God, and thou shalt interpret them,*
*with accuracy, and I shall give thee prophetic insight... saith the Lord.*
*And I shall give thee interpretation with accuracy, and I will use you,*
*and your wife in ministry. I shall use you as powerhouses in the Spirit.*
*...Archaeology! An Archaeologist in the natural, an Archaeologist*
*for the Glory of God. A Protector of the Ark. A Protector of Glory.*

This awesome word which the Holy Spirit gave me, you have learned,
as I share the discoveries of Ron Wyatt, you must have discerned.
For God supernaturally has intervened on mankind's behalf once again,
as the desire of God's heart, has always been for us with Him to reign.

# A SOLDIER IN GOD'S ARMY

Being part of God's army is such a great and intense honor,
as we wage spiritual warfare while raising our God's banner.
Putting on the whole armor of God into the raging battle we enter,
we are the sons and daughters coming from God's command center.

It's a raging battle because this is a daily spiritual war we fight,
we were drafted into God's army when we became His delight.
Accepting Jesus as our Lord and Savior, we now have the right,
by way of God's adoption we can claim our rightful birthright.

As we wage war in the front lines of the battle, we are safe,
for the battle is the Lords and He will keep us for His sake.
On the front lines, the only wounds found are self inflicted,
by those in God's army who His trust they have so restricted.

For we fight the good fight of faith, laying hold on eternal life,
as He hath called you out of darkness into his marvelous light.
As a soldier in God's army, remember while in the midst of war,
obeying God's direction and commands we must never ignore.

# A SPECIAL PROMISE FROM GOD

Not too long ago, the Lord called, chose and anointed me to preach,
His gospel through archaeology, for so many churches must I reach.
Through this prophetic gift, I can now separate the facts from fiction,
by His Holy Spirit, I'm able to avoid such forms of bible contradiction.

A special promise began, when He called me as His archaeologist,
in the natural and for His glory, in His presence I shall persist.
Ron Wyatt's mantle, God's has transferred onto my shoulders,
by His anointing, I can destroy those spiritual satanic boulders.

While praying at Glory Zone, a secret He said He would reveal,
for He promised me, the holy Ark of the Covenant I would feel.
Can hardly wait when God fulfills in my life, such awesome promise,
as I patiently await His most commanding voice, I won't dare miss.

To physically see and witness the fulfillment of His ultimate sacrifice,
Jesus shed His precious red blood on the cross, as the ultimate price.
As a witness to all, of the blood on the mercy seat of the ark exists,
the world better get ready, His supernatural love, none can resist.

# A TRIBUTE TO
# SUPERSTAR BILLY GRAHAM

There has been only one Superstar in the history of wrestling,
his name is Superstar Billy Graham, the only King of the Ring.
Just like Jacob as stated in Genesis, the first recorded wrestler,
as the angel of the Lord found out, God's man was a grappler.

Superstar was the man of the hour and the man with the power,
in the squared circle or out of the ring, just too sweet to be sour.
This flamboyant entertainer, who was truly ahead of his time,
such a remarkable career, he would achieve during his lifetime.

When the Superstar became the Wrestling Champion of the World,
he didn't know that one day his sculpted body would become so frail.
The effects of steroids in his body began to manifest in an unhealthy way,
realizing what he had done, repented before God when he began to pray.

As the Lord looked down from heaven and listened to his prayer,
would slowly restore his health and called him to be a demon slayer.
A warning to all you demons, principalities and princes of the air,
an awesome testimony and witness, the Superstar will surely declare!

Together with his beautiful wife Valerie, who's been always at his side,
what a tag-team combination, for no demon in hell could ever divide.
Such an honor and privilege to know this noble and spiritual warrior,
as the great Superstar acknowledges Jesus as his own Lord and Savior.

# A VIRTUOUS WOMAN OF FAITH

A woman that knows God is a virtuous woman of tremendous faith,
as she inclines her ear to God's own heart, she can hardly wait.
For true virtue cannot be earned but rather bestowed from the Lord,
a virtuous woman of faith, from her heart, her God she so adores.

A virtuous woman of faith seeks out the presence of the Lord,
as her passion for righteousness grows, Jesus is her reward.
She worships, prays and praises the Lord of His majestic traits,
as her spirit draws nigh unto Him, as a bride who hardly can wait.

A virtuous woman of faith is a vessel of honor, power and love,
her spirit, beauty and grace become as gentle as a beautiful dove.
For her meek and humble heart, searches for the word's holy truth,
she has been raised in the things of the Spirit since her early youth.

I am so thankful for my virtuous woman of faith that was God given,
for I also thank God, as our sins and transgressions, He's forgiven.
For my virtuous woman of faith is a psalmist and mother of two,
I admire her, as she worships and follows Jesus in hot pursuit.

# A WAR MOTIVATED BY LOVE

A war motivated by love, surpasses the understanding of men,
God continues to pour out His everlasting love, since time began.
Often, in the name of love, a person or nation must in war engage,
in the Bible, Iraq known as Babylon, history must turn a new page.

As the Iraqi people lived continually under their satanic oppressor,
Saddam Hussein has become the world's number one aggressor.
This nation from the very beginning, has always defiled the Lord,
their evil and corrupt governments are destined to die by the sword.

Throughout the world, millions of voices cried out for their freedom,
as United States responded to the threat of Iraq's old kingdom.
The declaration of war by President George W. Bush was in love,
most nations haven't realized, the order came from heaven above.

Our President George W. Bush believes in one nation under God,
motivated by love, as he responded in Iraq with such a mighty rod.
But please consider, often times it is the right thing to go to war,
as our heavenly Commander-In-Chief, to righteousness He's sworn.

# A WORLD VOID OF GOD

A world void of God would be much like living life with no hope,
a life without God's love, mercy and grace, Can anyone cope?
For the sad spiritual condition of this world, that we can measure,
how cultures around the world do consider their real treasures.

A world void of God becomes a sinful and a godless society,
for it would be very similar to living in a world, full of anxiety.
God who commands the wind, to bring us oxygen to breathe,
without truly repenting, sin and iniquity will continue to breed.

A world void of God, for Satan would surely overtake everything,
in Satan's sight, for his evil hatred for man won't stop quenching.
This whole world would be in an absolute chaotic state of mind,
until that day, when Jesus commands the devil to be confined.

Fear not, for the day of the Lord comes like a thief in the night,
as our Lord and Savior Jesus will not reject a heart that's contrite.
For whosoever shall call upon the name of the Lord shall be saved!
remember, a world void of God would be like just being enslaved.

# AN ARCHAEOLOGIST'S TALE

As I search and seek out natural landmarks,
throughout many countries around the earth.
To gather evidences as tales begin to unfold,
for the greatest stories that can now be told.

Acquiring artifacts from all over the world,
learning the languages and customs as of old.
There are so many books and records of stories,
some are facts and rumors of all kinds of glories.

To the land of eastern Turkey I did embark,
for down in the valley, I've seen Noah's Ark.
As I traveled to Israel through the Middle East,
did find brimstones but could not find peace.

Societies and cultures have many tales to tell,
of religious figures whom they all must hail!
Every civilization has someone they can trust,
eventually in the end, everything turns to dust!

# AN ENCOUNTER WITH CHRIST

I was brought unto this world, which I found full of darkness,
as I looked into the depths of my heart, I saw much sadness.
Is there any hope for me, since I feel like I was born to lose?
How can I live with purpose, many answers for me to choose?

In midst of self confusion and loneliness, I felt someone reaching,
it was like no one I have ever met before, just someone preaching.
God's word was being preached forth, as it began melting my heart,
my personal encounter with Jesus, understanding He would impart.

As He embraced me in His heavenly love, He cleansed me whole,
I have given my life totally to Christ for God to take full control.
My entire being belongs to Jesus, as I have given Christ my all,
I have gained everything from Jesus, as I have answered His call.

An encounter with Jesus Christ, forever will your world change,
born in captivity, He has set me free, no longer bound by chains.
If you ever encounter this man Jesus, do not let Him pass you by,
remember that if you ever ask Him anything, He will surely reply.

# ANGELIC HOSTS IN OUR MIDSTS

There are many types of angels, all of them in strength they excel,
those who followed Satan, became demons and will end up in hell.
An angel's wisdom and intelligence are supernatural and full of beauty,
as they serve, praise and worship God as their only heavenly duty.

We all have two ministering angels that follow us everywhere,
you may not feel them, touch them, nor see them with a stare.
Living in the real world, the one that the natural eye can't see,
these angelic hosts among our midst, do care for us with a zeal.

For their appearance can take on many different shapes or forms,
these archangels, cherubims and seraphims do superbly perform.
As they incline their ear to the spoken word of the Lord of Hosts,
these incredible angelic beings are different from demonic ghosts.

The great angelic hosts of the Lord God, are His holy messengers,
often deliver messages to those people, who are seeking answers.
You might of have entertained an angel by entertaining a stranger,
so be aware, that this could happen, even in the midst of danger.

# ANGUISH AT THE CROSS

Our Messiah Jesus anguish, began as the night began to darken,
as Jesus walked to Gethsemane, a place that was known as a garden.
His soul was exceeding sorrowful unto death: as the scriptures read,
for tarry ye here, and watch with me, Jesus of Nazareth had declared.

If possible, take this cup from me, Jesus prayed to the Father,
but nevertheless not as I will, but as thou wilt is what matters.
Jesus at the cross knew, as He suffered His greatest anguish,
for He had never experienced this type of inexplicable languish.

At the cross, Jesus suffered His worst and most painful moment,
must have felt like His most unpleasant and dreadful torment.
But on that peculiar day, the anguish of our Messiah had turned,
a pure flow of unconditional love for people, Jesus had yearned.

The anguish that Jesus suffered at the cross, can be described,
as a son who just lost His father, in His heart eternally inscribed.
The painful anguish was being separated from His Heavenly Father,
for He had never known nor experienced a more painful heart matter.

# ARE YOU SURE YOU ARE SAVED?

Are you ready to meet the Lord Jesus in heaven when you die?
Did you live the way you chose to live or the way God described?
If not sure, you most likely have chosen not God's holy way.
this means that you live a life of sin, for God you won't obey!

So my simple question still remains, Are you sure you are saved?
If not, well my friend, to be saved, the Lord Jesus you must crave.
Our righteousness is as filthy rags, His cleansing we are in need,
seek the Lord God with a pure heart and He will help you succeed.

Romans says; there is none that does good, none that's righteous,
Jesus stands knocking at very the door of your heart so courteous.
So we must lay aside every weight, and the sin which tears us apart,
and accept Jesus as our Lord and Savior, as His Spirit He will impart.

For whosoever calls upon the name of the Lord Jesus shall be saved,
as for our sins, offenses and transgressions, these Jesus has waived.
If you are not completely sure that heaven is your final destination,
you must believe in the Lord Jesus the Savior and His resurrection!

# AS THE SPIRITUAL BATTLE RAGES ON

The ongoing spiritual battle rages on between demons and mankind,
the earth is the battlefield were this battle has become entwined.
Our victory was secured and sealed, by the blood of God's son,
as we diligently search and seek in the things of God's kingdom.

For sin is running rampant throughout this selfish and dying world,
we cast out demons into outer space, where they have been hurled.
Although we win the war, while the ongoing battle is still raging,
using our weapons of spiritual warfare, we can send the devil ailing.

This is the very reason why the Church of the living God stands fast,
as the world will witness Satan's destruction by God's spiritual wrath.
For we boldly embrace the Holy Spirit's gentle guidance and leading,
His impartations into our frail hearts and spirit, He's been feeding.

As the church gathers spiritual momentum, and takes the offensive,
against the devil with his futile attempts, as he is on the defensive.
It's written, as the Bible declares that God's victory is totally ours,
the Lord Jesus defeated Satan, and stripped him of his powers.

# BEWARE OF GOD'S WRATH

The hand of our God is upon all them for good that seek him;
for remember the Lord God in all you do, and be free from sin.
But his power and his wrath is against all them that forsake him,
so repent, or the light that God has given you will grow so dim.

It's written, God's wrath comes on the children of disobedience,
let's all humbly walk in God's love as the children of obedience.
The fury and power of God's wrath is not a very pleasant thing,
for ungodliness and unrighteousness will God's wrath sure bring.

Often times, the wrath of the LORD against His people has kindled,
that's the time when His people must repent and their love rekindle.
For the mercy and grace of the living God is always at our disposal,
His everlasting love for humanity and loving care is just colossal.

There are numerous scriptures in the Bible, that speak of God's wrath,
do not forsake God, as you read these verses, please do the math!
Love the Lord thy God with all your heart, with all of your passion,
the essence and nature of the Lord God is love and compassion.

# COME UNTO ME, SAITH THE LORD

For come unto me, saith the Lord, as Jesus invites you in,
as He is so faithful to wash and cleanse you from your sin.
Since the second you were born, surrounded by sin's iniquity,
as the Lord's salvation has now become the believer's equity.

For the purpose of redemption, the son of God was manifested,
when man's human nature had horribly become so sin infested.
While He died at the cross, unto God, He has brought us nigh,
for that day we give our life to Jesus, His love He won't deny.

For come unto me, saith the Lord, as Lord Jesus calls you in,
He's always wanted and desired to dwell in us, from within.
As you come unto the King of Glory, just the way you are,
for He has always unconditionally loved us even from afar.

So come unto me, saith the Lord, just simply as you are,
for His name is also I Am, the only bright and morning star.
It is important for all to know, about the Lord's invitation,
He needs to put you through the process of sanctification.

# CONFUSION AT THE TOWER OF BABEL

As recorded in Genesis, it speaks of Nimrod the mighty hunter,
since the start of his kingdom was Babel, a tower of great wonder.
Located in the plain on the land of Shinar as written in Genesis,
its current location is in central Turkey, as Ron Wyatt insists.

At the Tower of Babel, men really thought heaven can be reached,
God totally did not agree with them, so He confounded their speech.
During that ancient time, the people's arrogance was their primary sin,
their languages confounded and couldn't communicate with their kin.

They wanted to make a name for themselves, as their vanity grew,
for the Lord scattered them abroad, for them to start their life anew.
These people who were one, now were upon the face of all the earth,
from that moment on, people from all nations and races were all birth.

The Lord God really hates man's dogma or religion, such a reality,
His heart truly desires a personal relationship with all of humanity.
This is why God the Father gave us His son Jesus for our salvation,
for He is calling a peculiar people to be His only and holy nation.

# CROSSING OVER INTO HELL'S COURTS

An ungodly wave of familiar spirit manifestations has been surfacing,
as the new television show known as "Crossing Over" begins airing.
The shows star John Edwards attempts to use his psychic powers,
as he tries to touch people's lives, deceiving them by the hours.

The premise of this show is that he can communicate with the dead,
yet the Bible condemns such behavior with any information that's shed.
In Deuteronomy it's recorded that this is an abomination unto the Lord,
consult not with these familiar spirits, for God must not be ignored.

For this type of manifestation of sorcery and witchcraft is not a joke,
never seek nor thirst after this for the Lord God you must not provoke.
The familiar spirits defile anyone who taps into this kind of behavior,
if you've sinned, just repent and asked forgiveness from the Savior.

Many people are whole heartedly fooled, mesmerized and astonished,
for those who engage in this practice, by God they will be admonished.
These ungodly familiar spirits, their counsel you must never entertain,
give your heart to the Lord Jesus Christ, and with Him you shall reign.

# DINOSAURS IN THE BIBLE

Most scientists today, say that about 140 million years ago,
dinosaurs lived and roamed throughout the planet, though.
When a giant asteroid slammed into Earth, was said,
was the true reason rather than Noah's flood instead.

Recorded in the book of Job from the Bible,
about Behemoth and Leviathan's true arrival.
These dinosaurs that the Bible does mention,
aren't just the words of a prophet's invention.

For the word dinosaur was born in the year 1841,
as the Bible says 6,000 years ago, for it was done.
Throughout many civilizations and cultures of old,
dinosaurs were known as dragons, we've been told.

Have you ever wondered if there were dinosaurs aboard Noah's Ark?
Yes, they were inside the ark; the long journey they would embark.
For Noah was intelligent enough to bring the baby ones on board,
two by two they came in the ark, working together in one accord.

We hear of recent sightings that have been reported,
the hunter who captures a dinosaur, will be rewarded.
Dinosaurs might still be roaming, remote areas of Earth,
they're very elusive animals, so take it for all that is worth!

# DISCOVERY OF NOAH'S ARK

From times everlasting to times of old,
about some forty four hundred years ago.
God spoke from Heaven and Noah He told,
make thee an ark, come and join the fold.

Two by two did the animals come to the ark,
what a long journey they would all embark.
For forty days and forty nights did it rain,
God's salvation was at hand and not in vain.

Upon the mountains of Ararat the ark rested,
from this point on, we have been created.
All our ancestors from one man they came,
as humans and animals are not the same.

This most awesome discovery a few years ago,
has made an impact for all of us who know.
I keep sharing the news with everyone I meet,
to God I hope all people will honestly seek.

# ESCAPE FROM SPIRITUAL PRISON

It is recorded in the Bible what Jesus said about,
deliverance to the all captives without any doubt.
Whatever your spiritual prison wall might just be,
trust and believe in Him, and He will set you free.

But the only escape route that has become available,
if you choose Jesus; your freedom will be obtainable.
If you reject Jesus, the devil's way you will choose,
for that chosen ungodly path, you will clearly lose.

Money is never a requirement for your safe escape,
truly loving the Lord Jesus, prison will you evade.
There is no spiritual prison that has walls so high,
for deliverance is at hand and surely draws nigh.

Get rid of those spiritual prison chains, once you're out,
praise and worship the Lord Jesus with a mighty shout.
Ephesians instructs us to put on the whole armor of God,
now you can live right while reigning with a mighty rod.

# FAITH MOVES MOUNTAINS

For faith moves mountains as the scriptures have so stated,
as Jesus dwells in our hearts, in faith we've been recreated.
Without faith, it is impossible to please the God of Creation,
faith is one of the cornerstones of our Christian foundation.

When you act upon God's faith in your own life as a believer,
He will raise you up among men as you become His achiever.
Is there a great mountain in your life that needs to be moved?
apply His faith in your situation, and see your life so improve.

A Christians act of faith, demands a response from our Lord,
just make sure your hearts are right or you might feel ignored.
Continue to pursue God and request your faith to be increased,
as He will decree, that your measure of faith will never cease.

For faith moves mountains as we pray the will of God today,
His answer could be on its way, but might encounter a delay.
The enemy is always seeking those, to whom he might devour,
since we are justified by faith, the devil lacks any real power.

# GOD HAS BEEN
# TARGETED FOR EXTINCTION

Most scientists claim that the dinosaurs on Earth went extinct,
about some 65 millions years ago, this point of view is so distinct.
Since there is no evidence whatsoever that supports this view,
I am here to uncover divine revelation, for all of you to review.

The only extinction I have seen, is the lack of understanding,
since man, does not truly understand that God is outstanding.
The devil is whole heartedly trying to separate God from man,
since from the very beginning of creation, when time began.

The love and reality of our Lord Jesus Christ seems to fade,
as this world were sin is embraced as man has been played.
Apparently, the devil has targeted God for total human extinction,
the onslaught continues against God, as man falls in deception.

Fret and fear not, for I give you great news in regards of this,
for Satan has been judged and his final destination is the abyss.
As God sits in control on His heavenly throne ruling and reigning,
through the Holy Spirit, for man's love He's still campaigning.

# GOD'S CALL ON MY LIFE

There's a call on my life for me to preach,
the Gospel of Jesus to all I must reach.
The biblical stories that have been recorded,
to them who believe in Him, shall be rewarded.

To those unbelievers I must share and tell,
how to go to Heaven and avoid earth's hell.
Ministering and educating to those who seek,
Be ye strong for in Him, thou are not weak.

Through archaeology our God has truly spoken,
His eternal mercy and eternal love is His token.
All the major biblical events so clearly speak,
of God's human intervention, I passionately teach.

I truly love this awesome call of God on my life,
that empty void in my heart, He's greatly satisfied.
As I preach through the science of archaeology,
His presence and existence is not mythology.

I must share with you, for all He has done,
throughout the ages since we've been born.
The Lord Jesus Christ my Savior is His name,
since He saved me, I have not been the same.

# GOD'S CHOIR DIRECTOR

On September of 1985, when Hurricane Gloria touched Long Island,
I auditioned for the choir, and became part of the church's bandstand.
Our choir, while caught up in worship, would reach heaven's heights,
together in one voice, we would become our heavenly Father's delight.

That spiritual experience was such an incredible life changing event,
as we touched heaven, the sacrifice of praises we would present.
Put on the garment of praise in exchange for the spirit of heaviness;
as it's written, Jesus is Lord and King, for our tongues shall confess.

While in the choir ministry, the Holy Spirit's anointing kept flowing,
Jesus would touch my heart and in God's knowledge, I kept growing.
For I am so appreciative for that special choir director over my life,
she would inspire and provoke me in love, to be as sharp as a knife.

I thank God, for everything my choir director in my heart did impart,
such deposit of faith from God's holy presence, I could never depart.
As she saw in me, so many things in God that nobody else would see,
I curse her current affliction, and pray that Jesus would set her free.

# GOD'S DIVINE NATURE REVEALED

As God's divine nature has been revealed through the ages,
He would send His only begotten son, as spoken in the pages.
The Bible does clearly reveal through His Holy Scriptures,
the Lord has painted such mighty and wonderful pictures.

As God's divine nature imparts pure and unconditional love,
while communing with His creation, being gentle as a dove.
The power to love and forgive rests on His mighty shoulders,
He's given us that same divine nature, as we obey His orders.

As God's divine nature through Jesus, unto this world revealed,
after Jesus died on the cross, forever our fate has been sealed.
Jesus is the express image of His Father as spoken in the Bible,
our faith and obedience in the Lord will determine our survival.

As God's divine nature entirely expresses His heart's true desire,
God's mercy and unconditional love towards us will never expire.
I pray that all men would come unto repentance before the Lord,
mercy and forgiveness have been poured out through His word.

# GOD'S EARTHLY THRONE

There's one place in the world, you can find God's earthly throne,
north of the Old City under the cross of Jesus, as His blood atone.
This location is known as Calvary, which is close by Skull Hill,
so Jesus did according to the prophets, the prophesy He fulfilled.

The general location in Jerusalem, The Garden Tomb is known,
who would believe this piece of real estate was British owned?
Surrounded by beautiful gardens, above is a Muslim graveyard,
also on the west side and close by, you will also find a vineyard.

God's earthly throne is none other than the Ark of the Covenant,
it always remained in Jerusalem since it never left the continent.
God's earthly throne by four angelic beings is heavily guarded,
there's simply no access, this area continues to be disregarded.

As the blood of Jesus from above the cross site, still lies there,
don't go searching for it, because you don't even stand a prayer.
Do not play around with the location of our God's earthly throne,
it's not meant for man to find it, as the Ark should not be shown.

# GOD'S GENESIS

In the beginning before time, when God spoke,
He created the universe in the midst of smoke.
The birth of the solar systems came into being,
such a magnificent sight, must have been seen.

As matter, time and space came all joined together,
by His spoken creative word, this can't get any better.
Since the Big Bang Theory wants to be violently heard,
folks, there's has never been anything more absurd.

Was the means through evolution or creation,
that some people are still asking the question?
Look up in the sky sometime today or tonight,
and behold and see the power of His might.

Sitting on His throne does God sit amazed,
the love for His people, sets Him ablaze.
For behold, it was recorded in His book,
for those who doubted, He never forsook.

# GOD'S GLORY ZONE

Where the Word gets preached with passion and authority,
a place where living holy before the Lord God is mandatory,
Where the pure flow of anointing forever more increases,
a place where unbelief and doubt get shredded into pieces.

At Glory Zone, is where our pastors preach with great power,
a place where true love overpowers as the enemy does cower.
Where our church wages war through anointed spiritual warfare,
a place where the captives are set free with fervent prayer.

Where people from all walks of life, freely come in,
by His Spirit, they're set free from the power of sin.
A place of comfort for spiritual restoration and healing,
God's mighty works and miracles are His daily dealing.

At Glory Zone, is where the godly revelation of giving,
is truly manifested by a cheerful heart of thanksgiving.
A place where God dwells by His awesome presence,
mercy and grace flow out from within His very essence.

God's Glory Zone, is a church where His love is clearly evident,
for the transformation of the unbeliever's heart is the evidence.
Our church has been patterned after the New Testament design,
for apostolic truth is what our pastoral leadership has defined.

# GOD'S GLORY ZONE: PART II

There is a church in Long Island, known as Glory Zone,
where the people of God, are reaching for God's throne.
Such a prophetic anointing throughout the world is known,
as God's people rejoice, for our sins has Jesus atoned.

The Holy Spirit seeks out the churches for His gift to birth.
for the prophetic anointing gift is a rarity among His Church,
As the Spirit searches those who seek Him with their heart,
touching their lives, as a new creation, a brand new start!

As Pastors Richy and Cathe Petrello spearhead God's move,
the principalities and powers of the air have been removed.
As the congregation in one heart and accord in Jesus unites,
taking dominion as kings and priests, for it is our birthright.

For here in Long Island, New York, there is a church sold out,
we worship and praise the Lord Jesus with a mighty shout.
Come visit us, bring your friends and family and get blessed,
and ask any one of us here, for we have a testimony to attest!

# GOD'S GLORY ZONE: TOTAL MEN 4 GOD

Whenever Glory Zone's Total Men 4 God get together,
there is no location in the Island that can get any better.
As we fellowship every Saturday morning in His name,
nobody who comes to our meetings ever leaves the same.

As we read, teach, preach and saturate in God's holy word,
growing in God, look not back but continue to move forward.
Encouraging one another, for the apostle Paul did instruct,
as the Spirit builds and molds us, He has begun to construct.

For the presence of God is such a blessing while we're united,
His sweet anointing is as evident as our faith becomes ignited.
The word of God gets preached with such power and authority,
with Almighty God on your side, you are part of the majority.

As the Total Men 4 God, our commitment is to serve our church,
to do whatever it takes, His presence we continue to research.
For as the followers of our Lord and Savior Jesus, we do submit,
that He's the King of Kings and Lord of Lords, and this we admit!

# GOD'S LAST EVANGELISTIC THRUST

In the last twenty seven years, every major event as recorded,
in the Bible has been identified, documented and discovered.
By an amateur archaeologist known by the name of Ron Wyatt,
a great "Man Of God" who was very godly, humble and quiet.

He discovered Noah's Ark, Sodom and Gomorrah, Exodus Route,
Mount Sinai Site, Crucifixion Site, and without a shadow of a doubt.
Ark of the Covenant, Death of King Tut and Red Sea Crossing Site,
the Lord has revealed the ancient secrets by the power of His might.

All these awesome discoveries, God has preserved and is presenting,
to everyone on this world, the devil has been busy misrepresenting.
Deceiving everybody in this planet about the reality of the Lord,
those lives that Satan has destroyed, Jesus will one day restore.

These last days, God has brought out His most powerful evidences,
His supernatural interventions on this planet are no coincidences.
The Lord of Creation still continues to reach out to fallen mankind,
for time is short, tomorrow is not promised so don't be left behind.

# GOD'S NAMES AND DESIRES

God has many names that He's been known throughout the ages,
these names can be found, by searching throughout the Bible's pages.
All the names of God in the Old Testament that have been revealed,
they all add up to the name of Jesus which God the Father has sealed.

In the very beginning, God revealed Himself to man as the Creator,
for one day, the Lord God would Himself come to earth as our Savior.
In the Old Testament God said; Jehovah was His personal name,
in the New Testament, Jesus and Jehovah are one and the same.

The Bible teaches that the name of Jesus, is above every other name,
Jesus was manifested to destroy the works of the devil as proclaimed.
Our Lord and Savior Jesus is referred to in the Bible in many ways,
for our Lord Jesus is worthy of all the glory, honor and our praise.

Who could ever imagine that God would want to dwell among us,
for in the beginning it was God the Creator, who made us from dust.
God has always desired in His heart to fellowship with His creation,
before time began, God put into motion His divine plan of salvation.

# GOD'S TRUE BLESSINGS

For many in the church love to hear about the God's blessings,
as all they care about are the things in their midst's of uprisings.
God's people often pursue blessings, instead of He who blesses,
the greater blessing is the one, who the person of Jesus possesses.

Many of God's people pursue the gifts, forsaking the gift giver,
the giver known as Jesus, is the one that His gifts, He delivers.
Always in the local assembly, the prosperity message is embraced,
but how the messages of sanctification will affect our own taste?

God's blessing closely follows your true commitment unto the Lord,
because He is worthy of all our praise and our life He has restored.
When you go searching through life for all types of natural awards,
know in your heart that Jesus is the greatest of all your rewards.

As the devil works day and night to deceive you with his delusion,
be fearless and brave as you remind him of his final conclusion.
If you take your eyes off Jesus, the devil will cause you to stall,
for our Savior Jesus Christ is the greatest blessing of them all.

# GOD'S WORD IS ETERNAL

Since the birth of creation, as written in the Bible's pages,
God has sovereignly spoken to mankind throughout the ages.
His word shall not return unto Him void, for it's very sharp,
we must embrace His holy words in the depths of out hearts.

So many counterfeits in the world, of God's word can be found,
but only one book has withstood the test of time, as so profound.
As the Holy Bible is truly the manual of the born again believers,
believing in God's only word, we become His unique achievers.

The Old Testament and New Testament are one single book,
as God shares His very thoughts, His people He has never forsook.
For His holy word is a lamp unto my feet, and a light unto my path,
I thank you 'oh Lord, because you have spared me from your wrath.

His second coming is near, but no one knows the time of His arrival,
for this barren and sinful land, God's sending His own wave of revival.
I close with this thought, sharing with you about the only Holy Bible,
the Word of God is the only thing we need to embrace for our survival.

# HOUSE OF PRAYER

For the house of prayer should not only be at the church,
as for every one that is called by God and has been birth.
A believer's home should be a house of prayer on demand,
with supernatural release of miracles, at the Lord's command.

A house of prayer exceeds the challenges of devilish works,
by God's intervention, making all devils look like real jerks.
As the people of God pray for their anointing breaking yoke,
their faith in their God, in His people, trust He shall provoke.

Pray through your dilemma or situation that seems hopeless,
God's assurance, for giving you the victory, you must profess.
Triumphant from afflictions, His greatness you can acclaim,
the sovereignty of the Lord, as His chosen people proclaim.

Prayer is the most powerful weapon in spiritual warfare,
that a born again believer, in God's holy name can declare.
As prayer reaches the heavens, of God's most holy throne,
while the devil and his evil kingdom get royally dethrone.

# IS YOUR HOUSE A HOME?

The Family that stays together in harmony and in love,
as they seek direction of the Lord from the heavens above.
As the house with Jesus as the center, becomes a home,
the still of peace and tranquility begin to reign, shalom!

For the family unit is so important in this very day and age,
keeping the unity in love, prevents anyone who would enrage.
Longsuffering and patience begin to develop in such a way,
as you set an example to your neighbors, such a great display.

The family that sows the seeds of peace and righteousness,
is the family where God gets glorified by the fruits it bares.
As the fruits of the Holy Spirit, will the Lord God increase?
Unto the family that sows love, the gifts will the Spirit release.

As for me and my household, the Lord God shall we serve,
for the house that is a home, His peace we must preserve.
One of the basic foundations of a home is God's holy word,
His laws and commandments we are all called to observe.

# ISRAEL ARCHAEOLOGICAL EXPEDITION

On March of the year 2002, I traveled to Israel in the Middle East,
staying at the YMCA Hotel in Jerusalem, I saw my faith increased.
Since my trip would only be for 7 days, I sure did carefully plan,
what a wonderful country I stood, in the middle of the Holy Land.

I researched the Garden Tomb area, where Jesus was crucified,
the tomb in this location is also believed were Jesus was buried.
Close to the Garden Tomb is located, near the Damascus Gate,
nearby, Zedekiah's Cave or Solomon's Quarry since it relates.

As I visited Masada's ruins and the Dead Sea area during the week,
the Cities of the Plain were clearly seen, since evidence I did seek.
The cities of Sodom and Gomorrah, their remains can still be seen,
the structures, thermal ionization and brimstones found from within.

As I walked and looked around the West Bank and the Old City,
my attention was captured to see people void of God, such pity.
Sadly such an incredible and beautiful city with such great history,
with so many archaeological sites to do research, full of mystery.

My research in the Old City of Jerusalem, such a magnificent site,
as I journeyed through the four quarters of the city, such a delight.
Jewish, Christian, Muslim and Armenian quarters were all together,
while visiting Israel, I prayed for peace and also for great weather.

# JUST FOCUS ON THE LORD JESUS

As Jesus Christ continues to be the focus of our journey,
we all gather together as one in His heavenly sanctuary.
The Father, Jesus and the Holy Ghost as one are united,
for we are His chosen people and we stand undivided.

As we continue to worship and praise our majestic Lord,
for Jesus Himself alone is King and worthy to be adored.
Follow the Master of all creation and receive His reward,
trust in Him and watch, as your whole life He will restore.

As Jesus Christ continues to be the focus of our being,
while resisting the devil, we continually see him fleeing.
For he tries to relentlessly deceive God's very own elect,
by God's decree, His Church, He has sworn to protect.

So let the mighty people of God rejoice in His Salvation,
it was always His plan from the start of earth's creation.
As we continue to focus on our Lord Jesus in supplication,
for our Christ and Messiah, deserves our total admiration.

# JUSTIFICATION BY FAITH

Justification by faith is based on the works of Jesus at Calvary,
since He shed His blood on the cross, this is the Bible's summary.
No creature on earth, could earn their way into God's salvation,
for your works and self righteousness, has no compensation.

You can't buy or purchase your way into God's throne in heaven,
from a works mentality repent or face God's wrath and mayhem.
There is no way of getting around the issue of God's justification,
because by being justified by faith, we can now resist temptation.

We're justified by faith, called by His name, this we do believe,
such an incredible gift that the Holy Spirit gives us to receive.
Faith plays an enormous role in a Christian's daily way of life,
so we don't have to struggle, as our spirit man becomes alive!

Our faith in our Lord Jesus should be our basic understanding,
for this should grant us to live life in manner that's outstanding.
Since we are justified by faith, I no longer live in tangible fear,
my faith in the Lord Jesus increases, as I continue to persevere.

# *KING TUT:*
# *PHARAOHS 1ˢᵀ BORN OF THE EXODUS*

King Tut, as he was affectionately known around the globe,
for this spectacular discovery has sent scientists into a probe.
As they all argue amongst themselves of how he actually died,
hidden, there's a powerful secret whereby man will try to hide.

For King Tut never reigned, since he was only a crown prince,
but the evidence that was uncovered, for a world to convince.
King Tut's cause of death in the book of Exodus, as recorded,
as the Lord commanded, Pharaoh's firstborn's life was aborted.

Amenhotep III has been clearly identified as Egypt's mighty Pharaoh,
for this was the last plague has brought Egypt an enormous sorrow.
The Lord God had commanded the death of all of Egypt's firstborn,
a great cry throughout all the land of Egypt, has caused all to mourn.

While the historians all argue about King Tut's father's true identity,
this inscription on a statue of a lion dedicated by King Tut is rarity.
In Egypt's Temple of Soleb, where he calls Amenhotep III his father,
for this Pharaoh also known as Thutmoses IV, did not die a martyr.

# LIFE'S DILEMMAS

As I'm looking at the condition of this world, it's sorrowful,
we are all in need of God's help to rely on the supernatural.
Apart from God, it is impossible to live life at its fullest,
without the Holy Spirit, your life will become the dullest.

You can't maximize your potential in life without His help,
for without Him, is like totally drowning in financial debt.
When it seems like there's no other option in life available,
Jesus is the answer to life's dilemmas, for He isn't a fable.

Confusion often attempts to settle in, into your own life,
almost like creating and birthing all kinds of tiring strife.
Born into a world, where iniquity seems to be rampant,
for almost every step of the way, life seems so militant.

Many of life's dilemmas just require the right resolution,
the way I see it, Jesus is the answer and the solution.
Our world seems to revolve on all kinds of confusion,
and once and for all, Jesus is the only known solution.

# *LIVING LIFE WITH GOD*

Living life with God, is like living full of grace,
God is such a blessing, He loves the human race.
His love never ends for His love is truly eternal,
compassion will keep me from the fiery infernal.

Can hardly imagine living apart from Him,
since Jesus was the only man who did not sin.
Life without knowing Jesus would tear my heart,
so I thank you my Lord, for the brand new start.

All our sins and transgressions are on His list,
by His blood and mercy they can cease to exist.
Listen to His grace for it acoustically sounds,
for His love continues and knows no bounds.

Before His presence I have chosen to live,
my sins and transgressions He will forgive.
That day, that His precious blood did spill,
by His love, all His promises He will fulfill.

Living life with God, should be the way of living,
in Him I have joy and a heart of thanksgiving.
So hear ye me, as I have shared from my heart,
my love for Him, no devil in hell will break apart.

# MAN IS GOD'S GREATEST CREATION

Although for His pleasure, we were so magnificently created,
over all the angelic beings, God has man graciously elevated.
Man was, and will always be by far, God's greatest creation,
it's my duty to remind Satan, that hell is his final destination.

Man, who is the express image of God, also has a living soul,
God shapes us on the potter's wheel, as He makes us whole.
Jesus as a man, so totally destroyed the works of the devil,
since the Holy Spirit's arrival, the playing field is now level.

By the blood of Jesus that was shed, His authority, He's given,
uh oh, bad news for Satan, for Jesus from the grave has risen.
So God has given us authority to put the devil under our feet,
Jesus conquered hell, death and the grave, as Satan retreats.

For the first man by the name of Adam, we were all born in sin,
it has always been God's heart desire for man to reign with Him.
The Lord God through His son Jesus has given us eternal life,
He shed His blood at the cross; His body, the ultimate sacrifice.

# *MAXIMIZE YOUR FAITH IN THE LORD*

Maximize your faith in the Lord, as the scriptures advice,
your life will be transformed, and this you won't despise.
As faith is the substance for the things that we do hope for,
for the evidence of things not seeing, unto Him we implore.

As a believer of the Lord Jesus, in Him we must always rely,
for all your wants and needs, He is more than able to supply.
According to His purpose and will, unto us He's commanded,
during times of great distress, He will not leave us stranded.

Maximize your faith in the Lord, as Jesus reigns forevermore,
as you seek Him fervently, His Spirit unto you, He will pour.
It's recorded that Jesus is the author and finisher of our faith,
this is the absolute truth, as there is no room for any debate.

The storms of life come knocking fiercely at your doorstep,
God sovereignly intervenes, the devil plans, He'll intercept.
So continue to rejoice in Him, as our Lord Jesus does reign,
for He is faithful and true, this we can certainly ascertain.

# MOVE IN YOUR GIFT

Move in your gift, as it was ordained before the world's foundation,
since they have been assigned to us since the beginning of creation.
For you have been called and chosen for the work of the ministry,
we are often being molded and shaped, just like vessels of pottery.

Every member in the body of Jesus, is been given a supernatural gift,
use wisely because the devil is scheming, as he's trying to be swift.
Your God given talents were given to you, for the body's edification,
and to help you resist and overcome the devil's ungodly temptation.

For God's gift in your life has been tailored made and very unique,
you must always remember that you should remain humble and meek.
The Lord always looks for earthly vessels, who Him will earnestly seek,
through the Spirit's talents and gifts, you may reach the highest peak.

You don't have to wait for no one to lay their hand on your head,
at the cross of Calvary, Jesus cried loudly, it is finished! He said.
Move in your gift that God has already in your life pre-arranged,
by the mighty power of the Holy Spirit, you have been ordained.

# MY FATHER WHO ART IN HEAVEN

My Father who art in heaven, hallowed be thy name,
for you alone are most holy and worthy to be praised.
Your majesty surpasses even the wildest imaginations,
thanks, for delivering us from all kinds of temptations.

As I deeply feel a sense of appreciation for my Father,
I know in my heart and soul, like you there is no other.
Your greatness destroys your enemies by your presence,
since no defense exists against any of the Lord's offense.

The attributes of Jesus are the express image of the Father,
If I'm rightly related to Jesus, nothing else will really matter.
My desire to please my heavenly Father becomes more real,
He continues to mold me, just like being on the potter's wheel.

It is so important to me, that my Holy Father must I please,
I will pray and seek His face; I humble myself on my knees.
For I sure hope that my sacrifice of praise, He will receive,
so I rejoice in the Lord as I'm saved, for this I do believe.

# OH' ISRAEL

A land of ancient realms and a land of majestic features,
its roots stem from biblical records, written by teachers.
Its real estate so intriguing, beautiful and heavenly divine,
for Jehovah God decreed that a Savior, He would assign.

A land, were the prophets and messengers were mistreated,
while this great nation lived in idolatry, living a life so defeated.
For the nation of Israel waxed strong in rebellion and pride,
the LORD God has spoken about salvation, He shall provide.

A land of great men and women, who were of God appointed,
as the Spirit of God came upon them, these were His anointed.
Many of God's people had prepared the way for His Chosen,
for unto the Lord's voice, the nation of Israel should hearken.

As the children of Israel were given Jehovah's commandments,
so that they would abide by God's law and avoid God's judgments.
Oh' Israel, why do you live and remain in your present condition?
I already sent my son Jesus to establish the "Great Commission".

# OUR FUTURE IN CHRIST

Our future in Christ Jesus was determined on Calvary's tree,
the blood that was shed by Jesus, we now have His guarantee.
Can't wait to worship and praise the Lord in those golden streets,
the day approaches when Jesus through us, the work He completes.

Our future in Christ Jesus, depends on our relationship today,
He's faithfully adopted me and mercifully washed my sins away.
Since our present spiritual condition will determine our outcome,
all authority has been stripped from the devil as he has succumbed.

Our future in Christ Jesus was never determined by the fall of Eve,
we as frail humans need God, as the devil still is trying to deceive.
Glory to God in the Highest, can't hardly wait to stand before Him,
for in that day, we will never be separated by condemnation or sin.

Our future in Christ Jesus, was pre-ordained before the foundations,
even before time ever began, and before the planet Earth's creation.
I imagine how glorious it will be, standing before His very presence,
we are the people of God, and in His name will gather in His essence.

# OUT OF LIFE'S RUINS,
# A GLADIATOR EMERGES

He was born in a midst of turmoil, the ruins of a broken home,
he grew and lived a life of confusion, void of love and feeling alone.
As a young man, his heart could never understand the lack of love,
that he would not know nor experience, but he was gentle as a dove.

This world could not offer any hope and while he couldn't find help,
not knowing about the salvation of Jesus, he was destined for hell!
One day, the Lord God reached for this man, for He did have a plan,
for this man accepted Jesus in his heart as his walk with God began.

From the ruins of a much hopeless life, as God would one day raise,
this man became God's Gladiator, with his heart, God he would praise.
For this spiritual gladiator would God one day call, choose and anoint,
As God poured his love and mercy to this man, He couldn't disappoint.

From the ruins arose God's Gladiator, as he began to understand,
this man's life was drastically transformed and changed by God's hand.
God's heavenly love, mercy and grace could this man now experience,
being saved and forgiven, this Gladiator could now walk in obedience.

# REACHING THE WORLD FOR JESUS

For Jesus spoke, to go into all the world and preach to the nations,
Christian believers should bring the good news to the populations.
To bring the gospel to the whole world was His commandment,
by His Spirit anointing we can pray through, and end the torment.

Reaching the world for Jesus, can be done with a heart of passion,
we minister in love to all generations, through the eyes of compassion.
We have been anointed to preach the gospel to the broken hearted,
by the fire of our hearts, we can get their own hearts jumped started.

For there are people's souls that are at stake on planet Earth,
the devil continues to work, trying to destroy their self worth.
So we must arise and be bold, give everyone the good news,
and intercede for them from the ongoing onslaught and abuse.

Let's not forget that Jesus loves and died for everyone's sins,
if you place your trust in the Lord, you cannot lose, but win.
By obeying the Lord's commandment, let's reach all the nations,
so that they may become part of the Lord's great congregations.

# RESTRICTED: THE KINGDOM OF GOD

For the Kingdom of God is certainly not available to everyone,
to gain access to God's kingdom you first must receive His son.
As sin prevents all of us from entering before His holy presence,
for righteousness, peace and joy in the Holy Ghost is His essence.

For the Kingdom of God will provoke you to live a life differently,
following the footsteps of our Lord Jesus, will change you incidentally.
Taking on the nature, mind and character of Jesus is not that hard,
you must decrease as He must increase, and sin you must discard.

For the Kingdom of God, the only access is through Christ's blood,
as God will raise up a standard when the enemy comes in like a flood.
Nothing on this earth can even remotely compare with God's kingdom,
So when we go to heaven, a mansion awaits us as our new home.

The Kingdom of God remains restricted, as access to most is denied,
as you must wisely choose life or eternal damnation, you must decide.
If you choose eternal damnation, sadly your destiny has been sealed,
but if you have wisely chosen God's eternal life, Jesus is your shield.

# SADNESS TO GLADNESS

One morning, on a cloudy and rainy day, a man woke up,
from a deep sleep he got up, began brewing his coffee cup.
This man started his morning wrestling with his own soul,
not realizing that his emotions were totally out of control.

Suddenly, the weight of the world, was on this man's mind,
he felt abandoned, as if everyone had just left him behind.
This man appraised his entire life before him and thought,
he couldn't figured out why he was feeling so distraught.

This man had noticed that, having lived for most of his life,
while thinking, realized also that he did not even have a wife.
So for all these years, this man has always felt lonely and sad,
later during the day, he prayed to God as he sought to be glad.

Some time on that evening he had found his mother's old Bible,
he began to read, not knowing, that God was sending a revival.
This man gave his life to Jesus, after the Gospels he had read,
and now he prays to the Lord Jesus, just before he goes to bed!

# SALVATION IS FOR EVERYONE

Since the beginning of man, God has wished that none should perish,
but that through His begotten son Jesus, that all would God cherish.
The Lord has lovingly spoken to all people, for salvation is at hand,
when you accept the Lord Jesus in your heart, is like love on demand.

For salvation has been made available to the gentile and for the Jew,
as God is not a respecter of persons, after His heart we must pursue.
We should all come to repentance, which is a gift from the Lord God,
humbling before Him, while eager to forgive us, while sparing the rod.

The Lord God has sovereignly provided Jesus as the sacrificial lamb,
believe me, because this is not a religion nor some marketing scam!
I'm speaking about a relationship with Jesus our Lord and Savior,
submit your life unto Him, and He will change your carnal behavior.

Whether you are American, Spanish, Jew, German or Japanese,
whichever nationality, take this opportunity and this moment seize.
For salvation is for everyone that is born from this planet Earth,
the blood of Jesus cleanses you, experience your brand new birth.

# SATAN'S DEVICES EXPOSED

Know, that Satan can transformed himself as an angel of light,
his satanic tricks and deceptions appear always to seem right.
But fear not, this prince of darkness has been judged already,
his final destination and the rest of his followers, as hell is ready.

There is so much sin and corruption in this diabolical being,
he swells in such arrogance, for his next victim he's foreseeing.
His hatred for the Godhead totally consumes and fuels him,
full of wisdom and perfect in beauty, Satan knows he can't win.

This created being known as Satan truly mankind he despises,
as he attempts day and night to deceive all with his devices.
Satan at one time, was the anointed cherub of God's creation,
he labors to separate man from God by the power of deception.

Satan is such a master of psychological and spiritual warfare,
for he was perfect in his ways from the creation days, be aware.
The good news: Jesus has conquered hell, death and the grave,
Satan can't be redeemed, but you can get redeemed and be saved.

# SAUDI ARABIA'S MOUNT SINAI

For hundreds of years, the world whole heartedly has perceived,
that the location of Mount Sinai in Egypt, as it has been believed.
Multitudes of pilgrims travel daily to the Sinai Peninsula to receive,
what's believed to be God's mountain, for the devil has deceived.

"For this Agar is Mount Sinai in Arabia", is what Galatians teaches,
in 1984, when Mount Sinai was discovered, NW of Arabia's beaches.
The highest peak in the region is a black mountain top charred by fire,
many other evidences can be found through the area, as we inquire.

Egyptian style altar with petroglyphs of cows and bulls can be seen,
the solitary tree on top and Mt. Horeb near, such an amazing scene.
Remains of twelve pillars can still be found in the vast majestic area,
looks like Ron Wyatt found the prophet Elijah's cave, right in Arabia.

The Saudis diligently trying to cover up this awesome discovery,
it ties them to the Hebrew nation, as they reject this uncovering.
Overwhelming evidences have surfaced, and can't be rejected,
to the world of archaeology, take notice, this can't be neglected.

# SEPTEMBER TEARS

As I sadly watch the Twin Towers collapse,
minutes seem like eternity as time elapsed.
I watched in disbelief over and over again,
my composure I tried so hard to maintain.

My sorrow had turned to September's tears,
this nation's hope had all turned to fears.
The impact of the lives that had been lost,
for death in Allah's name, at a horrible cost.

I will always remember those September's tears,
for a portion of sadness for the rest of my years.
The legacy of this great nation will always continue,
but this kind of religious horror must discontinue.

So much fear has been generated after so many years,
this event will always be known as September's tears.
For this country will never forget this dreaded day,
those people who are responsible will one day pay.

To all our heroes, who were born that peculiar day,
I salute you with all admiration in a very special way.
The people of this great country, in a state of dismay,
this sad event has provoked this great nation to pray.

# SONG OF THE PSALMIST

For the Lord Himself in the midst of His church, will sing,
as we lift our hearts in adoration, declaring Him our King!
The song of the Lord is a psalmist impartation of God's heart,
as we humble ourselves, His Holy Spirit from us will not depart.

The sacrifice of praise paves the way for God's holy presence,
love, mercy and compassion are the core of His very essence.
The congregation that reaches out for Jesus in such hot pursuit,
is a church that sings the song of the psalmist and breaks through.

The song of the psalmist prepares the heart for the Lord to hear,
He blesses those who don't give up, but in faith they persevere.
When the people of God sing unto Him, with their hearts ablaze,
as the devil cannot help it, as he becomes frustrated and enraged.

As the song of the psalmist seeks to magnify the King of Glory,
sing the book of Psalms and listen to such wonderful love stories.
For King David truly had a revelation of how to sing unto the Lord,
through his writings and heart, we see how much his God, he adored.

Michael Bonilla

# *STORMING THE GATES OF HELL*

In this dispensation of time, we sadly find the church asleep,
as the enemy comes in like a flood trying to scatter the sheep.
The time is surely approaching for the church to begin to arise,
the Lord God is going to deliver the church out of compromise.

As the Holy Spirit begins to increase the anointing and level of faith,
by storming the gates of hell until the spiritual enemy begins to fade.
We begin to surrender unto the Lord, as our hearts joyfully submit,
for Jesus will build His church, and unto heaven, us He will admit.

For too many centuries the devil has been roaming around the earth,
so now, the church is beginning to take her place, for what is worth.
Jesus at Calvary's cross, destroyed the works of the devil's devices,
the Holy Spirit is always there when the need of the church arises.

There are many ways to storm the gates of hell, for one is prayer,
through faith in Jesus Christ, for the other way is spiritual warfare.
But most important, you must keep your eyes focused on the Lord,
read your Bible faithfully, for God's word is like a two edged sword.

# SUCH A PRECIOUS GIFT

What a precious gift, for God to send His only son,
for when He died at the cross, He yelled it is done.
This precious gift is an impartation from God's love,
His wrath was poured on Jesus, from heaven above.

As we celebrate Christmas every December of the year,
let us greatly rejoice in happiness and also in great cheer.
For the things we receive, we should always be thankful,
as we trust in the Lord, let's believe and be prayerful.

What a precious gift, for the Son to rejoice over me,
I am the apple of His eye, as He's spoken and decreed.
This precious gift, is a revelation flowing from within,
I really can't wait to spend all of eternity with Him.

For God so loved this world full of sin and corruption,
His love for mankind has created such a disruption.
For that sinful devil, still cannot understand the light,
he refuses to acknowledge, the power of God's might!

# THE ANOINTED ONE

Jesus the Messiah, was also known as the one who was anointed,
for He was the one, that from the beginning of time was appointed.
The prophets of old, had prophesied and foretold of His soon coming,
a Ruler, whose goings forth, have been from of old, from everlasting.

The Anointed One was known as "Immanuel", it means God with us!
after His birth, He was named "Jesus", the babe who came to bless.
Jesus was 100% man and 100% God, as our sins He was to remove,
while crucified, He would shed His blood, for our lives to improve.

No one in the history of this planet, has mankind been so impacted,
by dying on the cross, love from His heavenly Father, He's imparted.
Many have come and gone, but never has man been so affected,
by the love of Jesus upon mankind He has sovereignly perfected.

Our Jesus has given us the greatest gift of all, which is life eternal,
He has also given His Holy Word, which is also His own journal.
Do what you can, get to know The Anointed One, for He's not far,
search and seek Him, and He will meet you, right were you are.

# THE ANOINTING OF THE LORD

Behold, the Spirit of the Lord has anointed me to preach,
for the Spirit has also given me the ability to boldly teach.
God's precious and anointed gifts are given without repentance,
through God's forgiveness, I can receive His very acceptance.

The anointing of God in my life, empowers me to go beyond,
His gifts are His to give, for His written word is His bond.
The Spirit of the Lord has called and anointed me to prepare,
ministering the gospel of His only son Jesus I will declare.

It's recorded in the Bible that the anointing breaks the yoke,
through the power of the Holy Spirit, His love, He will provoke.
Have you seen or heard? How the anointing sets the captives free,
by the blood of the Lamb and word of His power, Satan will flee.

Through the anointing of God's awesome Holy Spirit I say,
by pulling down spiritual strongholds of the devil as we pray.
Is any sick among you? The elders of the church, you must call,
prayer with anointing oil in the name of the Lord, for you all.

# THE ARK OF THE COVENANT

From Mount Sinai, the Lord God of Moses had spoken,
build me an ark, for my covenant shall not be broken.
For behold, I give thee my Holy Ten commandments,
my laws are eternal and will never see amendments.

The Ark of the Covenant shall carry my spoken words and laws,
if you love and trust in Me you will escape the enemy's claws.
As Israel's living God, I've decreed as the apple of my eye,
in those times of war, they only had to look up to the sky.

As the high priest would offer that one sacrifice a year,
all God required was that we become humble and sincere.
For as the blood was sprinkled on the ark's mercy seat,
Israel's sins were forgiven and they could know no defeat.

Today, the Ark of the Covenant represents God's earthly throne,
we as Christians have become God's heavenly and glory zone.
When Jesus was crucified at Calvary's cross just before He died,
Why have you forsaken Me? To His Father in heaven He cried.

At His time of death, a great earthquake and the rocks did rent,
the Roman centurion pierced His side, as blood and water was sent.
Behold, the blood of Jesus was spilled on the ark's mercy seat,
some day, this awesome evidence the world will one day see.

# THE BIBLE IS GOD'S HOLY WORD

There are so many books that proclaim to be God's holy word,
the Bible is the book that everyone should willingly prefer.
The Old and New Testament are both one book combined,
for God's own blueprints have been laid out for mankind.

Since The Bible is truly God's holy word that's inspired,
for the devil has worked very hard to against it conspire.
In his futile scheme to attempt to have the Bible destroyed,
but this evil device God foiled and the devil became annoyed.

Every word in The Bible was inspired by the Holy Ghost,
its truth and accuracy, no other written record can boast.
So many countless attempts to discredit these testaments,
as these prophetic writings have been purely heaven sent.

The spoken and written Word of God comes back not void,
so let's all that live on the earth rejoice and His plan enjoy.
For in The Bible you will find messages that spring forth life,
for those who reject God's words, He will spiritually smite.

# THE CHOSEN PATH OF THIS HEART

For the chosen path of this young and stubborn heart,
has been unfolding, for many years from the very start.
Born in a loving home, her own family she would betray,
her self-respect gone, as foolishness she would portray.

For the chosen path of this strong, prideful and troubled heart,
brought strife within her family, as her life had fallen apart.
She defiantly refused to hear the voice and word of the Lord,
godly words of wisdom from her family, she would so ignore.

For the chosen path of this hardened and so arrogant heart,
living and believing in her heart that she is virtuous and smart.
The strong and unconditional love of her family still remains,
oh God, please set her free from the bondage of her shame.

For the chosen path of this once stubborn and arrogant heart,
has repented before the Lord and His Spirit He will again impart.
She finally has embraced godliness and the counsel of the Lord,
pursuing the kingdom of Heaven and avoiding God's sword!

# THE CHURCH
# COMES OUT FROM THIS WORLD

When you do seriously look at the world's ongoing moral decline,
it's very obvious, that there is something wrong and truly not divine.
Can it be, that the inspiration behind mankind's lifestyle on Earth,
is purely and entirely based on his imposed value of his own worth?

During these trying times, where has the church been, all these years?
as the people of God prepare to pray and to shed some religious tears!
Amuse me. Has the church become the main problem in our society?
she satisfies her own lust and greed while gaining ungodly notoriety.

For God's people need to humble themselves, pray and seek His face,
don't live like the world does, void of God, like a church in disgrace.
God's mercy and grace is available for those, who from sin repent,
His church is called to be the very express image of God's presence.

It's time for the church to resume the posture of praise and prayer,
as we have been called and provoked to be spiritual demon slayers.
So awake and arise church of the Living God, set the captives free,
by the Holy Spirit's anointing, this is my plea, as the Lord decrees.

# THE DEITY OF CHRIST

With so many religions going to and from with confusion,
as so many regard the deity of Christ as a manner of illusion.
For the world religions become embroiled in their dispute,
rejecting the deity of Christ, for you must know the truth.

Throughout the Bible, the deity of Jesus is been revealed,
but you must search in the spirit, what God has concealed.
This understanding will come, by the Spirit of revelation,
you must ask God for the meaning of His interpretation.

As it is written that, Jesus said He was one with the Father,
He was nailed and suffered on the cross and died a martyr.
Jesus laid aside His deity to become a man clothed in flesh,
when asked about His deity, He couldn't deny, but profess.

It is also written, that Jesus was to be called "Immanuel",
as stated, the fullness of the Godhead in Him does dwell.
For the Pharisees during His day, just could not understand,
even today, this sentiment is found throughout the Holy Land.

# THE DEVIL'S STATE OF UPHEAVAL

As the devil comes to your house and begins to knock on your door,
by the power of the Holy Spirit, the devil you will totally ignore.
As demons maintain their untiring and relentless pursuit of total evil,
while ignoring and not understanding their current state of upheaval.

The devil conceived in his diabolical mind, a world he would control,
the Garden of Eden, from Eve and Adam, their dominion he stole.
For our heart attitude with revelation, unto the Lord we must extol,
as for the devil is like a roaring lion, seeking to destroy your soul.

As evil gathers together as one, such a state of chaos and confusion,
their schemes, devices and deceptions are his weapons of illusion.
For never in the history of creation, has any being behaved so erratic,
after the creation of the world, no one has caused so much static.

For lo and behold, our Lord Jesus Christ, has given us back dominion,
as He died about two thousand years ago, this fact is not an opinion.
As the devils current state of upheaval, by the day it so deteriorates,
the day is coming, as Jesus comes back, the devil He will annihilate.

# THE FALL OF LUCIFER

So, how art thou fallen from heaven, O Lucifer, son of the morning!
for the overwhelming arrogance and pride in thy heart was a warning.
You've seen God face to face, and to be worshiped you have desired,
and you deceived so many angels from heaven that you've acquired.

There is absolutely no shame found in you and no redeeming traits,
Jesus has prepared a hot place just for you, for hell violently waits.
For the wailing, weeping and the gnashing of teeth, you will partake,
as you get thrown into the furnace of fire, your soul, God will brake.

You did birth pure evil and are responsible for all of mankind sins,
Have you not read in Revelations, that the Lord and His church win?
You were cast down to earth by Michael the Archangel, as lightning,
this bad experience must of felt like your most horrible enlightening.

There is absolutely no sympathy, hope nor restoration to offer,
your treachery and despicable actions, for this you must suffer.
Thy greatest mistake was thinking that Jesus would surely die,
for one thing I know, is that in His holy love you will never abide.

# THE FEAR OF GOD TURNS TO LOVE

The fear of God is the beginning of wisdom,
reverence Him and be part of His kingdom.
The wisdom of God exceeds man's limitation,
He spoke and He laid the earth's foundation.

So fear God by keeping His just holy laws,
abide by His holy laws and live without flaws.
Keep my commandments if you love me, He said,
turn from me and you will be as good as dead.

I have wisdom; therefore I do fear my God,
when judgment comes He will spare His rod.
Fearing God acknowledges His power and strength,
His compassion and mercy reaches the fullest extent.

To the wise man who fears God with all his heart,
His everlasting love will He unconditionally impart.
Setting time aside, to worship the true living God,
by first fearing Him, He has turned my life in awed.

# THE FIRST MAN, ADAM

In the sixth day, from dust, Adam was God's first human creation,
after God's own image and likeness, Adam was the first generation.
No other human had been born nor conceived prior this first man,
in the beginning it was Adam and Eve starting their new life span.

The pre-adamic condition some Christians ignorantly believe in,
has no basis for biblical or scientific evidence as conceived in.
The Gap Theory predicts that people before Adam were living,
this flawed kind of assumed prediction is extremely misgiving.

The book of Corinthians says that Adam was made a living soul,
for the first day he was created, he was born completely whole.
Adam's intelligence as a man was unrivaled by no other being,
as Adam and Eve partook of the fruit, sadly both were agreeing.

In the sixth day of God's creation, Adam and Eve so masterfully made,
Lucifer in the form of a serpent would one day, their kingdom invade.
As the devil deceived Adam and Eve with a strong and sinful illusion,
God sent Jesus to destroy the devil once and for all out of his delusion.

# THE FLESH MUST DIE,
# FOR THE SPIRIT TO RISE

For the flesh must die so that the Spirit can rise from dust,
if you don't as a Christian, you will surely live in disgust.
The flesh continually wars against the Holy Spirit of God,
if you don't submit to God's will, the devil will your soul rob.

As the flesh tries and attempts to rise above God's authority,
make the righteous decision as your highest and holy priority.
For me, myself and I, are known as the ungodly trinity on earth,
cater to yourself and no one else, your destination will be death.

If the flesh refuses to die, we will remain just natural beings,
we'll engage in war against the devil, until we see him fleeing.
So don't be fooled, for these battles do occur on a daily basis,
these ongoing wars are no picnic and certainly are not an oasis.

The ongoing battle between the Spirit of God and man's flesh,
still continues to war until this day, as our spirit must refresh.
The flesh must be crucified in our hearts, so our spirit can soar,
we pick up our cross daily, and live for Jesus like never before.

# THE GENESIS CONDITION

Recorded in Genesis; about the giants of the earth in those days,
humans were so huge and tall, causing everyone to be amazed.
Unlocking the hidden keys to Earth's age, searching the mystery,
with the understanding of pre-flood times, let's dig into history.

For there was a canopy of water and or ice that covered the planet,
which prevented the harmful rays of the sun, on our bodies to reflect.
Since the magnetic field was so much stronger when time had started,
the oxygen intake was greater then, for now we breathe fainthearted.

For the planet's surface of God's new creation began void of rain,
temperatures all over the earth, had remained throughout the same.
Fruits, seeds and vegetables; the sustaining foods of God's choice,
such a beneficial wealth of healthy nutrients, made everyone rejoice.

The Bible clearly explains about the giants of the earth in those days,
imagine their size and weight during that time, a breathtaking display.
Mankind benefited from these extreme, rare and unnatural conditions,
the animals grew and became the dinosaurs during these transitions.

# THE HOUSE OF BONDAGE

In the book of Exodus we learned, what was the house of bondage?
It was literally a place where the people of God suffered abusage.
For the house of bondage on many Christian churches can reflect,
their idolatry and arrogance, for they surrendered their self respect.

Egypt was symbolic as the house of bondage for so many years,
for those hundreds of years did drive the children of Israel to tears.
The cause of God's people that lead them to this historical bondage,
was their worship of idols and a heart attitude on a violent rampage.

For many of God's people perished under Pharaoh's evil oppression,
since Israel had lost their understanding and their sense of direction.
A multitude of churches have assimilated a type of Pharaoh's house,
for many leaders in the body of Christ are acting just like a louse.

Thank God, that from bondage, the Lord God is bringing people out,
just like God did in the times of Pharaoh, through the Exodus route.
Any church that has become the house of bondage for God's elect,
unless you repent, your sacrifice of praise, He will certainly reject.

# THE ILLOGICAL GEOLOGICAL COLUMN

In the 19th century, Sir Charles Lyell was the one, who created,
as the so-called geologic column, from the rocks they had dated.
Scientists attempted to date the fossils by the rocks found in layers,
this gave birth to this theory of evolution, a known faith slayer.

Charles Lyell's published work was called the Principles of Geology,
such a great impact on Charles Darwin, with his degree in theology.
In 1859, The Origin of Species by Charles Darwin was published,
by means of natural selection, he tried to get creation demolished.

For the fossil record is the best evidence of Noah's universal flood,
and the lack of evidence determines the geologic column as flawed.
As stated by the non existent column, the sedimentary beds of rocks,
it can be found no where on earth, except in the school's textbooks.

I truly believe the geologic column is the bible of the evolutionist,
and these so called deceived scientists of evolution are delusionists.
For scientific methods and facts easily prove the flood's effects,
by the same standards, science magnifies evolutions real defects.

The geologic column periods or eras lack real scientific evidences,
for index fossils and circular reasoning are just fabricated pretenses.
With overwhelming evidences, wisely choose creation over evolution,
the theory of Earth's age being billions of years old, such an illusion.

# THE LAST DAYS AS
# RECORDED IN THE BIBLE

In many verses in the Bible you will find this famous saying,
as relating to "The Last Days", about the future's conveying.
Although this phrase is close to 20 centuries old as recorded,
those who have accepted Jesus as Lord, will then be rewarded.

For these last days will usher in, and bring forth perilous times,
were evil will manifest itself through man and all kinds of crimes.
Scoffers shall come in the last days, walking after their own lusts,
continue to mock God and His creation, for they shall be judged.

For God has spoken to us, through His Son Jesus, in these last days,
He reaches out for mankind to embrace His ways and not our ways.
As God prophesied that He will pour out His spirit upon all flesh,
through Jesus, His only begotten son, He'll take us out of this mess.

These last days have been taking place for quite some time now,
although the laborers are few, the harvest is ready to be plowed.
This dispensation of time, God is extending His mercy and grace,
to man, His greatest creation, to Him we must love and embrace.

# THE LORD IS ON YOUR SIDE

The Lord is on your side, so what's seems to be the problem?
for no situation or issue that's impossible for Him to solve.
Can anything be hard or too difficult for the Lord to take care?
there is nothing in this world that Jesus cannot Himself repair.

With the Lord on your side, you become part of the vast majority,
since everything in creation is totally subject unto His authority.
With Jesus as our advocate, we can spiritually soar like an eagle,
for the majestic attributes of our Lord God are so royal and regal.

With Jesus by my side, as I listen with my heart inclined to Him,
for now, my present and future have stopped from growing dim.
There is never a dilemma that the Lord won't remove you from,
He would never tolerate or allow your spirit to ever succumb.

With God the Father on my side, how could I ever feel alone?
He magnificently reaches and holds me, as If I was His own.
I so thank my heavenly Father, for Jesus and the Holy Ghost,
these three are one in the spirit, as I love these three the most.

# THE PASSION OF THE CHRIST

This motion picture promises to be one of the greatest of all time,
the Pharisees did accuse Jesus of Nazareth of such ungodly crime.
For the sin of blasphemy, our Messiah Jesus had been duly charged,
while the traditions of the religious leaders was tearing them apart.

The movie was so intense about how Jesus had been brutalized!
for Jesus was their true Messiah, and they still have not realized.
While in the midst of His people, Jesus the King of Glory stood,
in relation to the scriptures, the religious sect never understood.

Mel Gibson produced this wonderful and awesome masterpiece,
from the book of Isaiah it states that Jesus is the Prince of Peace.
Wounded for our transgressions and bruised for all our iniquities,
Jesus Christ has become the world's greatest of all commodities.

The main point of the movie was to show how much Jesus suffered,
as Satan thought that the link between man and God he had ruptured.
The greatest victory ever achieved was by a man who was despised,
oh' foolish devil did not know that Jesus on the third day would rise.

# THE PEACE OF THE LORD

Peace I give unto you, did Jesus speak to His disciples,
they were just not regular men, but God's chosen apostles.
The book of Isaiah speaks of Jesus as the Prince of Peace,
unto God the Father, He has made us kings and priests.

Proverbs says, but a man of understanding holds his peace,
knowledge and trusting our Lord, His peace He will increase.
God told Job to hold thy peace, and I shall teach thee wisdom,
for Jesus said to repent for at hand is heaven's holy kingdom.

It's written, that God's peace, which passes all understanding,
for Jesus shall keep your hearts and minds, that's outstanding!
Mark wrote, have salt in yourselves, and peace one with another,
for the Lord Jesus, is a friend that sticks closer than a brother.

Galatians decrees that peace, is one of the Spirit's fruits,
for a stem of Jesse, and a Branch shall grow out of his roots.
Jude wrote, mercy unto you, and peace, and love, be multiplied,
for the peace of our Lord will be established soon... worldwide.

# THE RESURRECTION POWER OF JESUS

Whatever the situation or circumstance might possibly be,
know that the fact of the matter is that there's a guarantee.
That Jesus Christ rose from the grave, as the Bible decrees,
there are three that bare record in heaven, all as one agree.

The resurrection of Jesus is the most documented event ever,
this glorious event's reality has so impacted history forever.
Since the beginning of time and earth's supernatural creation,
behold, as for this would open the doors to mankind's salvation.

In Jerusalem, Israel, there's physical evidence that was uncovered,
for the empty tomb of Jesus, in the 19th century was discovered.
Many people saw Jesus alive some time after His resurrection,
the history books record this earthly and heavenly celebration.

In this day and age of the 21st century, we are still witnesses,
the inspirations created by God, as He unfolds His purposes.
The resurrection power of our Lord Jesus is relevant for today,
for no greater act of love for mankind, has ever been displayed.

Michael A. Bonilla

# THE RISE AND FALL OF JUDAS

While Jesus traveled in Jerusalem, looking to set an example,
He walked up to Judas Iscariot and called him to be a disciple.
Judas for more than three years would fellowship with Christ,
he would often witness miracles and the power of Jesus might.

Judas himself had been given by Jesus, authority over devils,
he grew closer to Jesus, spiritually he'd reached another level.
Judas was a thief who only thought about himself and no other,
for Jesus truly loved Judas, even like His own natural brother.

After knowing Jesus for approximately three and a half years,
Judas would betray Jesus, and would never shed a loving tear.
As the spirit of greed grabbed a hold on Judas the deceiver,
he turned on his only friend Jesus, for thirty pieces of silver.

For the small amount of money, the former disciple received,
Judas Iscariot didn't realized, he had been royally deceived!
It had been prophesied long ago, that Judas would rise and fall,
for it would have been better if he would never been born at all.

84

# THE SAD STATE OF WORLD RELIGIONS

For the sad state of world religions are in such dismay,
most are not rooted or grounded and in total disarray.
The essence of these religions magnifies the separation,
between man and his maker, the Lord God of Creation.

The sad state of world religions are so void of God's truth,
misleading people from all nations from the start of their youth.
Written records do not match those, to the Bible's scriptures,
as truth and error are combined as religions own mixtures.

The affairs of the world religions are the cause of strife,
they indoctrinate people with fear, for the rest of their life.
For these people do not know God's holy and inspired word,
obviously the Gospel of Jesus Christ, they have never heard.

But thank God, for He is dealing with all the world religions,
from all the continents, to all the cities, from all the regions.
This sad state of world religions before God they shall bow,
all who are responsible, the Lord Jesus will totally disavow.

# THE SEARCH FOR THE TRUTH

As you search for truth and look everywhere you can,
seek the Lord God, and He will guide you with a plan.
The word of God declares and also provides the proof,
recorded throughout the gospels that, Jesus is the truth.

Many false messiahs have surfaced in the last centuries,
all these ungodly people belong in hell's penitentiaries.
Many false prophets will proclaim the word of the Lord,
all these will also die by God's sword and His holy word.

Since the word of God and His truth are one and the same,
His name is Jesus the Messiah, as the devil turns insane.
For his hatred towards the Son of God, grows even greater,
the day cometh as Satan, will bow his knees before his creator.

For the truth is certainly out there, but do you know where?
Just seek God's holy word, and you'll see Him everywhere.
So fear not, for once you find Jesus, you'll stop your search,
for you will also find Jesus in the midst of His local church.

# THE SECOND COMING OF JESUS

The second coming of Jesus, will be the greatest event,
the world will ever experience from His heavenly descent.
As foretold from the voice of the prophets, of His return,
those not walking in God's will, you should be concerned.

For when Jesus Christ arrives on this ungodly planet earth,
He will come with His saints and His holy angels to unearth.
The seeds and fruits of man's sins and evil transgressions,
for thousands of years, have left their evil impressions.

As the rapture of the church of the living God draws nigh,
when all of God's holy saints on earth, will look up in the sky.
Jesus will establish on this old planet, His heavenly kingdom,
on that day, the devil will be chained as he gives up dominion.

If you read this poem and are not part of God's family now,
behold, every tongue shall confess and every knee shall bow.
Recorded in the scriptures, to the Glory of God the Father,
because if you're not saved, nothing else will really matter.

# THE SECRET OF THE GARDEN

For the Garden Tomb is believed to be were Jesus was buried,
He shed His blood on that rugged cross with love that He carried.
It was written that Christ had been crucified next to a garden,
He died for all of us whose hearts had been born so hardened.

In one language it was known as Golgotha, the skull's place,
were one day, our Savior Jesus would pour out His grace.
And in another language, this location was known as Calvary,
for this man Jesus Christ was much more than extraordinary.

For this location, Jesus redeemed us back to God the Father,
in this garden, He stood single and alone above every other.
North of the city wall in Jerusalem, there's a very special site,
in this garden, He was buried for three days and three nights.

But the most important fact about this great and incredible story,
is that Jesus Christ who died and resurrected, went up to glory!
Through His death and resurrection, He has gathered us to safety,
please don't forget that this borrowed tomb, He left it empty.

# THE STORY OF MOSES

He was raised in Egypt, but was born from Hebrew parents,
as he grew up, he would become a man of many gifted talents.
Being well versed in Egyptian culture and military knowledge,
his wisdom, the people throughout Egypt would acknowledge.

For this young Hebrew man's name was none other than Moses,
he became God's man, years after the death of Jacobs's son Joseph.
These symbols known as hieroglyphs, someone should decrypt,
as one day, the God of the Hebrews called Moses out of Egypt.

God told Moses to lead God's people from the house of bondage,
as the Lord was preparing for a showdown, at Egypt's final stage.
When Moses led the children of Israel through the mighty Red Sea,
the Lord parted the deep waters, for His people to witness and see.

Upon Mount Sinai, the children of Israel themselves had gathered,
where God handed His holy laws unto His people, which mattered.
As Moses walked with God, for in everything in Him he depended,
for this great man Moses, was also the one that Lord God befriended.

# THE STORY OF THE CITIES OF THE PLAIN

Recorded in the Bible's book of Genesis from the Old Testament,
were these five ashen Cities of the Plains that are on document.
Zoar, Admah, Zebohim, Sodom and Gomorrah to name these five,
as it rained fire and brimstone nothing there could ever survive.

From out of heaven, did God send His righteous judgment?
Those cities and the plains went up in smoke, such torment.
As Lot's wife looked back and became such a pillar of salt,
for no one is to blame, for this was plainly her own fault.

Although, these cities had been turned into burnt dust,
this example has been given to us, for God we must trust.
I've seen these cities, for they still can be seen today,
Just travel to Masada, Israel, and see the remains this day.

Today, the remains of these cities, can still be distinguished,
for this culture, civilization, and life had been extinguished.
The evidences of fire and brimstone can still be clearly seen,
the vast damage caused by thermal ionization make such a scene.

For these evidences in detail have been documented and recorded,
by loving and obeying His commandments, blessings will be awarded.
So let the story of The Cities of The Plain be an example to all,
by His love, mercy, and grace, even you can be standing tall.

90

# THE TRUTH ABOUT LEVIATHAN

Of all the animals God ever created, among them there is one,
who is the fiercest dinosaur ever known to man under the sun.
The Bible in the book of Job, of the mighty Leviathan it speaks,
for this one particular animal, not one scale of his body is weak.

In ancient times throughout history, as a dragon he was known,
and his mighty power was even greater than that of a cyclone.
Leviathan's name refers to no other than the Tyrannosaurus Rex,
on Earth, this most incredible dinosaur structure is most complex.

It's amazing how the Bible, Behemoth and Leviathan it mentions,
it almost feels like this is a story, right from the fourth dimension.
Throughout the fossil record, the T-rex bones are most distinct,
for this mighty dinosaur known as Leviathan, still remains extinct.

In the book of Job, it's recorded that Leviathan was fire breathing,
as this amazing dragon, had the unique ability of smoke exhaling.
Upon this Earth, there's no one like Leviathan, who is without fear,
if you ever happen to meet up with Leviathan, you better disappear.

# THE WATERS OF THE RED SEA

The silent waters of the Red Sea hold a most powerful mystery,
for God destroyed Pharaoh's army, for this is Hebrew history.
The actual location of the remains of Pharaoh's army was found,
chariot cabs, wheels and spokes can be seen were they drowned.

For the Red Sea crossing site took place in the Gulf of Aqaba,
and this site is east of Egypt and directly west of Saudi Arabia.
Sadly, in the map sections of all Bibles, this information is not,
forgotten long time ago, seems like this is part of the devils plot.

As the Lord God truly had hardened Pharaoh's stone cold heart,
the Red Sea waters contain many physical evidences of chariot parts.
For the miracle of the Red Sea, which the Lord God had commanded,
a sign of love towards Israel, for their obedience He has demanded.

As the Lord God, who brought Israel out of the house of bondage,
out from Egypt's land and from Pharaoh and his army of savages.
There might be a Red Sea in our lives were God wishes to deliver,
from the bondage of sin, God's love and mercy flows like a river.

As the waters of the Red Sea hold evidences of God's deliverance,
He wills for us to serve and freely love Him without any hindrance.
For God has purposed in His heart for us "His people" to in Him rely,
He has poured out all His love on us, as He patiently awaits a reply.

# THE WAY OF THE REDEEMED

The way of the redeemed is the understanding of who's their Savior,
once you become part of the family of God, you will have His favor.
Since you have been bought and purchased at a very costly price,
please allow me, to give you some glorious and heavenly advise.

To know the way of the redeemed, you must accept Jesus as Lord,
for His ultimate act of love on the cross, must not ever be ignored.
As Jesus Himself became as sin before the Father's very own eyes,
Jesus said to His Father to forgive them, just before He would die.

As Jesus hath redeemed us from the curse of God's very own law,
as He was made a curse for us: this event, many witnesses saw.
For the Bible does say, cursed is every one that hangs on a tree,
when Jesus resurrected from His cold grave, what a day of jubilee!

The way of the redeemed, is really knowing what Jesus accomplished,
since the powers and forces of hell, Jesus has completely demolished.
As the Lord Jesus on Resurrection Day, defeated death and the grave,
Glory to God, for His redeemed will never again be the devil's slaves.

Michael A. Bonilla

# THE WHOLE ARMOR OF GOD

As we humbly pray before we engage in spiritual warfare,
we are prepared to serve notice on the enemy, we declare.
The book of Ephesians tells us to put on God's whole armor,
for the devil is ready to be stripped of his apparent glamour.

For the ongoing battle cannot be fought in the natural realm,
through hope, truth and righteousness, the devil we'll overwhelm.
These daily battles, must always be fought in the spirit world,
through faith and across the galaxies must the enemy be hurled.

Destroying the works of darkness, through the armor of God's light.
flowing in the anointing of the Holy Spirit, we're ready to fight!
For setting the captives free from their spiritual confinement,
while in battle armor, demolishing demons is our assignment.

Putting on the whole armor of God, has been His provision,
we should carry out and execute this spiritual military mission.
Now that we are able to stand against the wiles of the devil,
since Jesus resurrected, the playing field has been leveled.

# THE WOMAN IN THE FIELD

A certain woman in the field, her pain she tried to conceal,
she asked God about her affliction, would she ever get healed?
I approached and asked her, how long she's been praying for?
she answered, for a few days now, as she woefully implored.

I asked the woman, why are you so happy and not disappointed?
she replied, God said, He would send a man that was anointed.
As I leaned over and laid my hand over her head and did pray,
I spoke to her and said, peace be with you and don't be afraid.

I felt virtue flow out through me and unto her body so frail,
the impartation of healing virtue in her body would so prevail.
She got up and screamed unto God, such a deep expression,
for God had answered her prayer by lifting her depression.

So she turned and thanked me from the bottom of her heart,
she continued to rejoice for God had given her a new start.
I was asked, what was I doing in the field in the first place?
I heard your prayer, I replied, and brought you some grace.

# THE WORK OF THE MINISTRY

The five-fold ministry has been given to us for the saints perfecting,
for in the name of Jesus, the works of the devil receive the impacting.
During the works of the ministry, we see the equipping of the saints,
by power of the Holy Ghost, the saints will not be weary or faint.

For the edifying of the body of Christ, becomes our God's top priority,
the saints of God have been pre-ordained, under the Lord's authority.
He gave some, apostles, prophets, evangelists, pastors and teachers,
these gifts that the Lord has given us, they benefit of all creatures.

Are you involved in ministry of your local church that you attend?
If you seek God's heart and purpose, He'll help you comprehend!
As He searches not for spectators, but rather the participators,
to become heirs with Christ, for like Him, there is none greater.

It's such a great blessing and honor to do the work of the ministry,
many are called and few are actually chosen, as for this we agree.
For we encourage one another in the things of God, as we rejoice,
as we come together to worship Jesus in one heart and one voice.

# THERE'S A STORM COMING YOUR WAY

For behold, you better be ready, God is sending a storm this way,
so if you are not right with God, you must repent and begin to pray.
For no one can stop this storm, because is the Lord God sending it,
so humble yourselves and seek His face, to His Holy Spirit submit.

Is there already a storm in your life? Could it be several storms?
Well, there's mercy, love and grace that's available, I must inform.
You must get rid of all kinds of hidden sins and transgressions,
by repenting with a humble attitude, direct to God all confessions.

We may not be able to prevent the storm that God has decreed,
As He is seeking to destroy the works of the devil to set you free.
If you are right with God, He will spare you from the incoming storm,
as you get closer to the heart of God, your life He will transform.

God's wrath might be concealed through the storm that is coming,
believe in the Lord Jesus, and your victory will be so overwhelming.
Behold, judgment starts in God's house and His church He will purge,
as He promises, a glorious church without spot or wrinkle will emerge.

# TOUCHING THE
# HEART OF GOD WITH MUSIC

Before time began, God created music for His heavenly pleasure,
to worship and praise Him is greater than any earthly treasure.
You can minister music to the heart of God, through natural things,
the call to minister music is greater than those of angelic beings.

God's music imparts and touches His love to every heart,
there's nothing on heaven or earth that is of a higher art.
To adore God with music is what I really want to express,
there is no one greater in the world more worthy to bless.

With instruments and vocal sounds to heaven will I send?
there is no one in this universe who's a greater friend.
I clap, dance, sing and shout unto the Lord with all my might,
through my faith, the inner depth of His heart I hope to incite.

Music, is such an awesome way to stand before His presence,
His unmatched and unconditional love is His very essence.
For behold, no weapon formed against you shall ever prosper,
with music and faith, I hope to touch the heart of the Master.

# *TRANSFORMED*

Being born into this world as my journey in life starts to begin,
living life not knowing who God was, is like falling into sin.
But, thank God, that one day from out of His mercy and grace,
for God lovingly and kindly would reach out for me to embrace.

For ye shall be not conformed to this world, as written in Romans,
but be transformed by the renewing of your mind, as it cleanses,
To prove what is that good, acceptable, and perfect, will of God,
this transformation of our entire being, as part of God's squad.

Also beware and don't marvel for Satan himself is also transformed,
into an angel of light, ready to deceive all, so be not misinformed.
The fallen angel is out there recruiting people from all walks of life,
so that he can keep you also in the darkness away from the light.

The most powerful by far, the transformation of our human heart,
that transition from the depths of darkness, as from evil you depart.
The path is very narrow into the glorious entrance of God's kingdom,
perhaps a place prepared in heaven, a mansion that we can call home.

# WHEN GOD OPENS A DOOR

For God is about to open the kind of door, that no man can shut,
the enemy tries to intervene, to become the cause of distraught.
At times, when God closes a door, He also will open a window,
as provision comes from Him, this you must understand and know.

Often times, the Lord has to impart patience in your stressful life,
if God doesn't intervene, you would feel surrounded by nature's strife.
The Lord chooses at will, to open a door on your behalf and benefit,
for by His spirit, you have full access to God, not needing a permit.

For no man has the power to close the door that God has just opened,
and no demon has the authority either, since they've been cautioned.
Now listen, you may be going through some turmoil even as you read,
know that you are destined to win, so get yourself ready to succeed.

If it seems that God has sort of forsaken you, trust not that voice,
as the enemy speaks of everything but the truth, so in Jesus rejoice.
For God would never leave, nor forsake you as recorded in scripture,
we look forward for the day, that we all get caught up in the rapture!

# WHEN THINGS
# DON'T SEEM TO GO RIGHT

When things don't seem right and apparently are not well,
while nothing turns out right, you feel like saying farewell.
You attempt to enjoy life, but you seem to be under a spell,
it so feels like you are not living on earth, but rather in hell.

Fortunately, there is a solution to every care of this world,
even if it appears that your life has been thrown in a hurl.
Relax, for the Lord is faithful to those who in Him believe,
for in all things trust God, and unto Him you must cleave.

I can certainly understand what you must be going through,
your victory lies on the King of Glory, who you must pursue.
For many are the afflictions of the righteous, as recorded,
but the Lord delivers them out of them all, as He ordered.

When things still don't seem right as you would so perceive,
beware, the devil is out there against you, trying to deceive.
For the Holy Spirit's anointing on your life you must receive,
take heed, for your breakthrough, you shall surely achieve.

# WHO IS THE HERO?

For so many claim in this world to be so called heroes,
when it comes down to it, they are nothing but zeroes.
But there is only one person that qualifies for the title,
and His name is Jesus and He's the only that is entitled.

Often people proclaim other people and name them heroes,
as if they were a type of comic book character or superhero.
Our world is not built on the notion of fantasy, but of reality,
but it seems that this notion is the expression of the mentality.

You will have heroes birth from people in the natural realm,
through their circumstances and courage will overwhelm.
As written, every good gift comes from your heavenly Father,
for our Lord Jesus, He is the true hero and like Him, no other.

So all you false and self proclaimed heroes of this dying planet,
repent from all this self imposed glory, before you greatly regret.
The world's only and true hero is our very own Lord and Savior,
and His name is Jesus, so you better be on your best behavior.

# WHO IS THIS JESUS?

This man Jesus is sitting on the right hand side of God the Father,
as Jesus is the only begotten son of God, like Him, there's no other.
In Isaiah, it refers to Him as the Wonderful Counselor, Mighty God,
Prince of Peace and the Everlasting Father as He rules with a rod.

The impact of the birth of Jesus, caused earth's calendar to change,
the scholars implemented a new system for the dates to re-arrange.
Never in the history of mankind, has one man made such an impact,
ancient history texts from all over the world verify this awesome fact!

Much more than just a prophet, and not just an ordinary mortal man,
Jesus and Jehovah are the same, for He is also the I AM that I AM.
As the Lamb of God who takes and removes the sin from the world,
also as the Lion of Judah, and in the book of John, He's the Word.

Now, this is the Lord Jesus, who died for our sins at Calvary's cross,
as the Lord Jesus our Redeemer, has shed His precious blood for us.
Thank God, that on that third day, Jesus did resurrect from the dead,
as God's master plan continues to unfold, such a testimony lies ahead!

# AUTHOR'S AWARDS AND RECOGNITIONS

Michael A. Bonilla, Ph.D.

1. Submitted in August of 2002 the poem "The Ark of the Covenant", which was recited at a Symposium and Convention in Washington D.C., sponsored by The International Library of Poetry. It was attended by 1,600 poets and more than fifty countries were represented.
2. Nominated "International Poet of the Year" for the years 2002, 2003 and 2004.
3. Inducted as an International Poet of Merit and Honored Member of the Society for the years 2002, 2003 and 2004.
4. Winner of the International Poet of Merit Silver Award Bowl for the years 2002, 2003 and 2004.
5. Winner of the Commemorative Award Medallion for the years 2002, 2003 and 2004.
6. Awarded twice the "Editor's Choice Award" for the month of September of 2002 and for the month of December of 2003.
7. Semi-finalist on October 11, 2002, in a poetry contest sponsored by American Poets Society.
8. Third time, semi-finalist in the International Open Poetry Contest sponsored over the Internet by the International Library of Poetry (www.poetry.com), for the years 2002, 2003 and 2004.
9. Second time, semi-finalist in the Poetry Contest sponsored by Famouspoets.com and Friendly Poets for the years 2003 and 2004.
10. "God's Creative Touch" poem selected to be recorded on *The Sound of Poetry* album collection, to be released both on compact disc (CD) and cassette tape versions.
11. Selected for publishing, in the Anthology titled *On the Wings of Pegasus*.
12. Selected for publishing, in the Anthology titled *Eternal Portraits*.

13. Selected for publishing, in the Anthology titled *Letters from the Soul*.
14. Selected for publishing, in the Anthology titled *Whispers*.
15. Selected for publishing, in the Anthology titled *A Moment to Remember*.
16. Selected for publishing, in the Anthology titled *Songs on the Wind*.
17. Selected for publishing, in the Anthology titled *The Days Unraveling*.
18. Selected for publishing, in the Anthology titled *Patterns of Life*.
19. Selected for publishing, in the Anthology titled *Words to Remember*.
20. Selected for publishing, in the Anthology titled *On the Wings of Poetry*.
21. Selected for publishing, in the Anthology titled *The Best Poems and Poets of 2002*.
22. Selected for publishing, in the Anthology titled *A Celebration of Poetry*.
23. Selected for publishing, in the Anthology titled *The International Who's Who in Poetry*.
24. Selected for publishing, in the Anthology titled *Our Most Famous Contemporary Poets*.
25. Submitted in March of 2004 the poem "*Angelic Hosts In Our Midst.*", which will be recited at a Symposium and Convention in Reno, Nevada, on September 4 of 2004, sponsored by Famous Poets Society.
26. Winner of the Shakespeare Trophy of Excellence for 2004.